The End of Self-Doubt

Build Lasting Confidence and Self-Esteem
with the Inner Compass Method

Marc J. Sachnoff

The End of Self-Doubt
Build Lasting Confidence and Self-Esteem
with the Inner Compass Method

ISBN-13: 978-0692287002

Published by
Modern Wisdom Press
a subsidiary of
Enlightened Enterprises, LLC
Kirkland, WA

Printed in the United States of America

First Printing, 2014

Contents

Dedication

This book is dedicated to my wife Lynn, who has put up with my unusual intuition experiments for all these years; to my parents for their endless and unconditional support; and to my mentor in life, Dr. Daisaku Ikeda.

As soon as you trust yourself you will know how to live.

– Johann Wolfgang von Goethe

Introduction

Why Read This Book?

T he End of Self-Doubt is the result of over 20 years of research and experimentation aimed at understanding the simple premise that you, and every single person on this planet, have the innate ability to guide yourself towards health, happiness, and fulfillment. In this short book you will learn how to achieve real clarity so that you can move forward with confidence in every area of your life.

Imagine what your life would be like if you had no doubts, no second-guessing, and no susceptibility to scams. What would it feel like to have rock solid confidence in your decision-making ability? What would your business and personal relationships be like if you could discern the true intent of the person in front of you? What would your life look like if you were taking steps towards creating excellent health, joyful relationships, and financial abundance?`

Sounds great. But you're probably wondering, "If I have the ability to achieve all this in my life already, why isn't it happening?" I'd suggest that the main reason is self-doubt, rooted in years of disempowering programming, starting when we were children.

We consciously and unconsciously buy into this programming, and it has robbed us of the ability to confidently take command of our own lives. The good news is that it can be undone. Self-doubt can definitely be transformed into self-love and self-confidence.

This may sound like a tall order, but I guarantee you that you have what it takes to become an inner-directed person who can not only live a joyful and fulfilling life, but also play an important role in transforming our society for the better—all by learning to access your inner wisdom.

How can I make such a bold statement? Because I've worked with over 300 people—ranging from 14 to 85 years old—and all of them were able to access this higher self.

So if you want to learn how to trust yourself, access your inner wisdom, turn on your inner GPS, and navigate successfully through this challenging world, then this might just be the most important book you will read all year.

The process I'm going to teach you is not magic. It does not rely on a supernatural, external "Other" to grant our wishes or give us special knowledge—although who wouldn't want a little help from a genie or a fairy godmother now and then?! Or at least someone like Mary Poppins to drop in, clean up our messes and make it all better. But the truth is, Mary Poppins and Tinkerbell ain't coming. We have to deal with life ourselves. And like all things worth doing, this process will require time, patience, and practice to learn and master. But if you are willing to try, even just dip in a toe or two, I promise that you will discover a world of possibility unimaginable to most people.

It's never too late to end self-doubt and begin trusting yourself.

So let's get started!

Note: This book is full of experiments to help you practice the techniques being shared. You might find it helpful to keep a journal as you go through these experiments to help you track your progress.

Prologue

An Encounter with
the Buddhist Yoda - Part 1

W hen I first started practicing Buddhism, I was suffering from a series of agonizing health problems: awful digestive issues, terrible migraines, and disgusting sinus infections. My stomach was constantly bloated and I fluctuated between constipation and diarrhea. In short, I was a mess.

I went to doctor after doctor but all they could determine was that I had Irritable Bowel Syndrome— which basically means your digestion isn't working right, but they don't know why. I visited chiropractors, nutritionists, and acupuncturists, to no avail. On top of everything, I had a high pressure job in TV and two young kids at home. I was truly miserable. So a friend suggested I go see an older man who had been practicing Buddhism for half a century. My friend called him "The Buddhist Yoda of Los Angeles." Intrigued, I agreed.

A few days later I found myself seated in front of this person. He did, in fact, look a bit like Yoda and he even talked a bit like Yoda too. I listed off all my problems, and once I finally finished my lament, I expected him to share some profound Buddhist wisdom. Instead, he smiled slightly and said, "Why don't you go home tonight, open your refrigerator, place your hand on each item and ask it whether or not you should eat it."

I looked at him like the confused dog in the cartoons; my head shaking violently from side to side. "What?!" I blurted out. I had never heard of such a thing.

He smiled again, this time using his hands to illustrate his instructions. "When you go home tonight, open your refrigerator, and place your hand on each item and then ask it whether or not you should eat it."

I looked at him incredulously and responded, "Okay..."

That night I went into the kitchen, making sure my wife and kids were all asleep. I opened the refrigerator and took out a jar of something and immediately the idea came to me to hold this jar against my gut. After all, that was where I was having the most consistent problems. Then I asked myself, "For my highest good, for my greatest health, should I eat this?"

And you know what? I got an answer.

Then one night about a week later, I found myself back in the kitchen, peering inside the fridge. We'd hosted a kid's birthday party and dozen six-year-olds were passed out on the floor in the living room. Inside the freezer was the leftover half of a Baskin-Robbins ice cream cake. And it was Mint Chocolate Chip, my all-time favorite.

Suddenly I heard my wife call out from the bedroom, "What's going on in there? It sounds like you're having a fight with the fridge!"

She was right. Without realizing it, I had been arguing with myself— out loud.

While I was really craving that cake, I was also getting a powerful inner signal to NOT eat it. I was getting a clear message that the three major components of the cake—wheat, dairy and sugar—were the primary causes of my headaches and digestion problems.

My wife continued, "Whatever you're doing in there, you better stop it! You're starting to freak me out!"

So I pulled my hand out of the freezer and shut the door.

And just like that, a new chapter in my life had begun. As I continued to listen to this inner wisdom, what I now call my Inner Compass, my health began to steadily improve – and so did many other aspects of my life. Now I want to share what I've learned with you in the hopes that you can derive as much benefit from this work as I have.

�֎

Chapter 1

They Taught It, You Bought It!

W hether we know it or not, whether we like it or not, most of our internal operating system was programmed by other people. So much of how we live our lives, how we make decisions, choose friends and lovers, buy products, pick our clothes, vote, invest our money, and even think about ourselves is the result of years of conditioning.

Parents, teachers, ministers, grandparents, brothers, sisters, and friends have all had a hand in creating the person we are today. And we are also constantly getting messages from the media—through TV, books, radio, YouTube, magazines, Facebook, blogs, and websites— telling us subtly, and not so subtly, what to wear, how to act, what to think, and who to be.

If I were to write a song about this, the refrain would go something like:

They taught it...

You bought it...

But what is your essential truth?

There are a lot of people in society (big business, the media, government, etc.) who have a strong interest in controlling who you are and how you act. They want you to be good boys and girls, good students, good employees, good patriots, good consumers, and good soldiers. And that means not rocking the boat or asking questions.

But there are a few problems with this plan:

1. They didn't ask your permission, and
2. Their plan is not working for the planet (see: global climate change, economic inequality, police brutality, etc.) or likely for you as an individual.

So it's time to make your own plan. And in order to make your own plan, to chart your own course, you need a compass: something that will guide you un-erringly in the direction of your greatest happiness. You'll learn all about it in a later chapter, but for now let's focus on becoming aware of all the programming and conditioning that we have been exposed to every day since we were born.

Researchers tell us that as a child you are bombarded with 40,000 product messages[1] a year. Then you head off to school where you are expected to conform to a certain pattern of behavior—and if you don't, you'll be judged "a slow learner," a "trouble-maker," or a "problem child." You discover that if you wear certain clothes or talk a certain way, the other kids will call you "stupid," "stuck up," "trashy," or any number of names. So you learn quickly how to fit in. And the fastest way to fit in is to conform to the norm—whatever the governing norm is—regardless of whether it's healthy, loving or life-enhancing for you or anyone else.

Sound familiar? And if you don't learn how to fit in... well, there's an old Japanese expression that the nail that sticks out gets hammered down first.

By the time you get to high school you are either part of a well-defined peer group or feel like an outcast. Anyone who has felt like an outsider knows the pain of longing to join the "in group". And if that seems impossible, we dream of moving to a new city to start over, unburdened by the labels heaped on us by others. But as adults, inventing a new persona isn't an option—especially if you have gotten married,

---

1   http://pediatrics.aappublications.org/content/118/6/2563.full

had kids, taken on a mortgage, and are juggling a demanding job, a family, and a mountain of debt.

But it's never too late to start being true to yourself.

By the time I turned 16 years old, I just couldn't handle it anymore. My parents had gotten divorced, I hated high school, and the limitations of my environment and my own low self-esteem had become an intolerable prison. I took a bold step and arranged to graduate early after the summer of my junior year with the intention of joining the Peace Corps. The high school administration agreed to this plan before I discovered that you have to be 18 to qualify for the Peace Corps. So instead, I headed to New Orleans to study jazz.

New Orleans was a strange and untamed oasis in the midst of the still repressive south. Plus it was dirt cheap—a Coke was a dime, a pay phone call cost a nickel, the trolley was a quarter, and you could get a big plate of steaming hot red beans and rice in the French Quarter for under a dollar. Add a big andouille sausage and you could eat like a king for a buck and a half! And New Orleans was full of people from around the country who were, like me, in the process of either discovering or re-inventing themselves. I fit right in.

It was in New Orleans that I began to discover that much of who I thought I was had been dictated by others. My new friends were jazz musicians, cooks, conmen, street dancers, professors, recovering Confederates, amateur chemists, strippers, and gamblers. The steamy summer nights were filled with long alcohol-fueled debates about the nature of reality, consciousness and the meaning of life. Among this island of broken toys was an old hippy who happily scavenged food off dirty plates at restaurants, stole from everyone he knew, and lied so easily that lying became his truth.

I'd never met such a scoundrel before in my short life. I was outraged and disgusted. Then I went back to my tiny room and was unexpectedly confronted by my landlady, a large woman whose sugary drawl barely concealed a powerful temper which was now aimed full force at me.

"You lying little shit!" she yelled at me, waving my driver's license in my face. "You told me you were 18 but this says you're barely 17. If the city found out I was renting to a minor I could get shut down. What other lies have you be pulling on me?!"

What a delicious juxtaposition I found myself in. I had been railing about what a jerk my liar acquaintance was, but here I was merrily altering the truth myself. And now I'd been caught.

I won't lie to you, I was crushed. And in spite of my desire to look strong, I started to cry. My giant landlady, who seemed to fill the entirety of that hot, tiny room, softened a bit. "I'm not gonna mama you boy, I'm gonna wean you. When you open your mouth to me it better be filled with the truth!"

I spent a very raw night alone with myself. What is the truth? Why did I need to lie to people?

And then I had a valuable but unpleasant realization: all people lie. Kids learn that grownups lie. Grownups see other so-called adults lying—often brazenly—on TV, in print, at work, at home, etc., and think, "If everyone's doing it, it must be ok."

I thought lying was just part of life. But I rationalized that when I did it, it was for good reasons, whereas when the scoundrel did it, it was reprehensible. That brought me to big, but unpleasant realization number 2: not only do we all lie, but we justify our lying with our own twisted version of morality.

This makes trusting other people a real challenge.

Yet most of us have at least a handful of people in our lives to whom we have given our trust. To examine the concept of trust in more detail, I invite you to try the following activity.

What to do now:

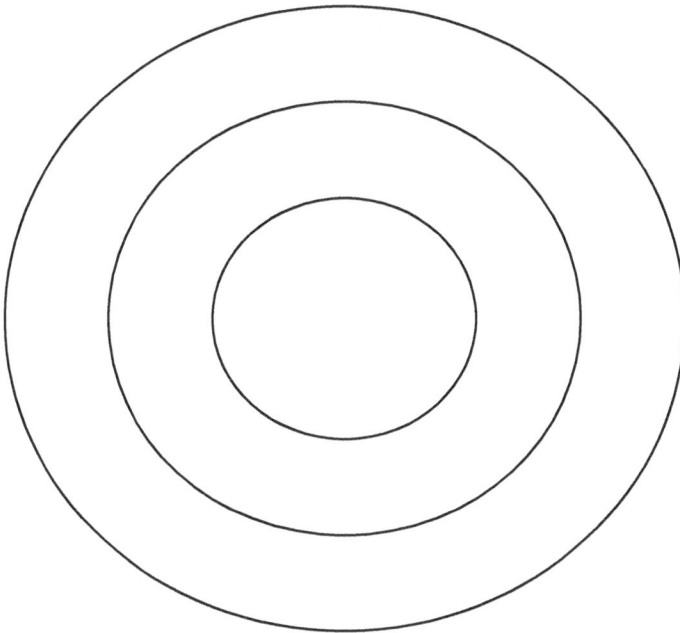

Figure 1. Circles of Trust

Identify circles of trust

The diagram in figure 1 contains three circles. In the center circle, write the names of the people you trust wholeheartedly. These might be friends or family with whom you share your hopes, dreams and darkest secrets. We know these people will protect our privacy, and would never let our confidential conversations become public knowledge, appear on Facebook or be shared with our ex. If you have more than two people in this innermost circle, you're doing better than many people on the planet.

In the second circle, write the names of people that you have a strong level of trust in. These are people you'd trust to take care of your kids and you wouldn't hesitate giving them a key to your house or your car. But you wouldn't necessarily tell them everything about your life. Note that there may be some crossover between folks in circle number 1 and 2.

In the outer circle, write the names of people you have a moderate level of trust in. These might be friends, family, co-workers, or members of your church or other community. You might not have room for all of them, but we're just looking for a representative sampling. Beyond these three circles is, well, everyone else on the planet.

We'll be coming back to this page later on so take the time now to complete it before moving on.

So how did it go? Was it difficult to think of people you trusted?

Trust in Society

Statistically speaking, starting with Watergate and Vietnam and dramatically accelerating with the Iraq invasion and the financial meltdown of 2008, public confidence in key institutions in our society has plummeted. The level of trust that exists between individuals and the institutions that my parents and grandparents relied upon – mostly without question – has deteriorated to the point that I'm worried about the very survival of our democracy.

And I'm not the only one. The National Conference on Citizenship released a report in 2012 measuring confidence in public institutions and warned:

"An erosion of confidence in major institutions of society, especially those of a representative democracy, is a far more serious threat to democracy than a loss of trust in other citizens or politicians... [L]oss of confidence in institutions may well be a better indicator of public disaffection with the modern world because they are the basic pillars of society. If they begin to crumble, then there is, indeed, cause for concern"[2].

Think about it. 50 years ago, a doctor's word was sacrosanct. But despite the many well-intentioned people who enter medicine, nowadays we are bombarded with stories of overtired physicians, underpaid nurses, misused drugs, unnecessary operations, abandoned patients, unsterile environments, and botched procedures. As a result, many of us have simply lost faith in doctors and hospitals.

And hey, I'm not just picking on the medical profession. Recent Gallup Poll data indicates the deterioration of trust between citizens and societal institutions is widespread[3].

Take education. When I was in school, if there was a problem—and believe me, I caused plenty of problems in school—my mom would side with the school and against me 100% of the time. No questions asked. Nowadays, the situation has flipped. I recently spent two years working with an education reform group aimed at empowering families. Most parents told me that if there is ever a problem at school, they automatically side with their child, not the administration. What's the reason for this 180 degree turn? Parents no longer trust teachers, they don't trust administrators, and they sure don't trust the school district.

According to a national poll conducted in 2012, Americans generally have less confidence in the public school system than they did 40 years ago. Gallup reported that only 29% of Americans had "a

---

2   http://www.ncoc.net/Confidence-in-Public-Institutions-OKCHI12
3   http://www.gallup.com/poll/1597/confidence-institutions.aspx

great deal" or "quite a lot" of confidence in public schools nationwide, exactly half the confidence level reported (58%) in 1973[4].

Ask yourself: which of the following do you trust?

- the military
- your church/religious community
- the public school system
- the media
- the advertising industry
- the auto industry
- Hospitals, Doctors
- the pharmaceutical industry
- the judicial system
- the banks
- Wall Street
- the police
- the FBI, the CIA
- Congress

Unfortuntely, the news is filled with stories of people who have been let down, cheated and betrayed by these organizations[5].

What about the news itself – do you even trust the press? It's hard to tell what is actually news anymore, now that facts are so frequently distorted to fit whichever narrative is most convenient for politicians and corporate sponsors.

The bottom line is that many folks simply don't believe that these groups — which have traditionally formed the foundation of our society — have our best interests at heart. Therefore, they don't deserve our trust.

So who can we trust? Well, I wouldn't recommend looking to celebrities or athletes for moral guidance either. Two words: Lance Armstrong. Need I say more?

---

4   http://www.ncoc.net/Confidence-in-Public-Institutions-OKCHI12
5   I recognize and appreciate the efforts of good and sincere folks working within these institutions. But the behavior of the organizations as a whole has hardly been confidence-inspiring.

But if we can't trust athletes, celebrities or institutions, then who can we trust?

I would submit for your consideration that before we can begin to rebuild trust in our society, we first need to trust ourselves. By that I mean we have to be able to turn off self-doubt and develop our own judgment, discernment, and wisdom. This is no small task. In fact, I've been working on this for over 20 years. However it can be done. I have concluded that there is a fundamental, unchanging, and essential truth within each of us: a powerful tool you can use to help guide you successfully through life's most challenging times.

And I want to help you discover that essential truth.

Chapter 2

Finding Your Essential Truth

Not to get all spiritual here, but having recently celebrated my 30th year of Buddhist practice, I've spent a lot of time contemplating the idea of an essential self common to all people. The Buddha taught that all living things inherently possess an essential enlightened nature that is one with the enlightened nature of the Universe. This means that, no matter our age, gender, race, religion, ethnicity or social status, we all share an unchanging, fundamental truth.

From a scientific perspective, there's a lot going on inside and outside our bodies that we don't perceive. For example, right now, millions of cells in your body are cooperating to move your muscles, pump blood, digest food, pull oxygen from the air into your lungs, convert chemicals into fats and sugars, and connect ideas, memories and sensory experiences together in your brain. To list all the processes that are occurring inside your body at this very moment would require a book in itself.

But who, or what, is conducting this extraordinary symphony of life? Just as pre-enlightenment thinkers believed the sun and stars rotated around the earth, we have been conditioned to believe that everything in our lives revolves around our conscious mind.

Don't get me wrong, a lot of our life does revolve around our conscious mind—the part of you that is actively reading this sentence, deciphering these symbols and considering their meaning, for instance. But the conscious mind is just one part of the whole system.

For the sake of this book, and for the experiments you will be doing along the way, I'd like you to consider for a moment that there might be several other aspects involved in making you *you*. On a molecular level, we know that our DNA acts like a blueprint for our biological development. On a psychological level, thanks to Sigmund Freud[6], we know that our unconscious mind (including subliminal thoughts, habits, repressed feelings, hidden phobias and desires) also shapes our behavior. Fellow psychoanalyst Carl Jung[7] postulated that we are also influenced by the collective unconscious—which contains all the memories, images (archetypes) and experiences of not just our own lives, but our entire species. Add in all the confusing messages and conditioning we have received every day since our birth and you begin to see just how complex human beings really are.

But don't get caught in an existential crisis just yet. The whole purpose of this book is to help you discover your inherent wisdom and confidence— the safe harbor that has always existed inside yourself— which is in harmony with the most positive aspects of the universe, spirit or god.

To do so, we need to access another kind of consciousness—the non-linear, creative part of ourselves. This knowledge sometimes manifests as gut feelings, hunches, mother's wisdom or intuition.

Dr. Gerd Gigerenzer, Director of the Max Planck Institute for Human Development—and source of much of the underlying material in Malcolm Gladwell's book *Blink*—has a lot to say about intuition. His research[8] shows that people have been tapping their intuition since the beginning of humanity and in many cases use it as "the steering wheel through life."

---

6   http://www.britannica.com/EBchecked/topic/219848/Sigmund-Freud
7   http://www.britannica.com/EBchecked/topic/308188/Carl-Jung
8   *Gut Feelings: The Intelligence of the Unconscious*, Dr. Gerd Giggerenzer, Viking 2007

Specifically, Dr. Gigerenzer says an intuition or gut feeling refers to a judgment:

1. that appears quickly in consciousness
2. whose underlying reasons we are not fully aware of, and
3. is strong enough to act upon.

While intuition can sound esoteric and ancient, it's part of the daily life of millions of people around the planet. Even Steve Jobs told us he used his intuition to help make Apple the global success it is today, but he didn't tell us how.

I believe our intuition is a deep, internal knowing. I call it our Inner Compass. I believe we all possess inherent wisdom—a connection to God, Jesus, Buddha, spirit, body wisdom, a oneness with the universe... whatever name you prefer. This is a deep knowing of what is right for us at any moment, and a different kind of intelligence than most of us were taught to cultivate. Regardless of our education or background, I am confident that all human beings possess this capacity.

Accessing this inner wisdom is kind of like discovering a new gear in your car that you didn't know was there, but can really power your life forward. Harnessing this inner wisdom is the fastest and most effective way I know to overcome self-doubt and become the master of your own destiny.

Anyone can do this. You may not get it right off the bat, but I can assure you that after working with hundreds of people, every single one of them was able to access their Inner Compass. And so can you—if you want to.

This may resonate with other meditation practices or self-help techniques you've tried before. You might immediately feel comfortable with this or you might worry about looking silly or sounding crazy—that's ok. Just go with me for a bit and see what happens. If you approach this work with an open mind and an open heart, you might be surprised at what treasures you can discover inside yourself.

But before we can begin to access this inner wisdom, I want you to think back through your life to see if you have already had an intuitive experience.

What to do now: That funny feeling

Answer these questions as honestly as you can:

- Have you ever experienced synchronicity that was hard to explain logically?
- Have you ever been overwhelmed by a sense of familiarity (déjà-vu) when going somewhere or meeting someone for the first time?
- Have you ever thought about someone just moments before they called you on the phone or showed up at your door?
- Have you ever had a strong feeling telling you not to do something or not to meet someone?
- Have you ever had a strong feeling telling you to take a certain route while driving, or embrace a specific option when facing an important decision?
- Do you ever have gut feelings, mother's intuition or strong hunches?

✦

Chapter 3

Turning Off the Inner Critic

T he biggest obstacle most people face in accessing their Inner Compass is not lack of ability. As I mentioned, I believe the ability to tap our inner wisdom or Inner Compass is standard equipment for all human beings. It is patiently waiting for us to turn it on— like a Porsche or Ferrari sitting quietly in our garage. The main obstacle that prevents people from reaching their full potential is what I call the Inner Critic.

Oh, that dastardly voice in our heads. The one that pipes up when you're trying on that stylish new outfit and sneers: "You're too fat to wear that!"

A friend calls this the Itty Bitty Sh*tty Committee. Another friend calls it his Inner Board of Directors, because they are always ordering him around. Yet another calls it her Evil Twin, while some Buddhists call this the Monkey Mind. Whatever you call it, the Inner Critic is the voice of self-doubt, disbelief, disempowerment, distrust, disgust, and just about every other negative descriptor we can think of.

Have you ever caught yourself thinking:

- I'll never be able to afford that
- She will never love me
- I don't deserve that raise
- I'll never amount to anything

- They don't really like me
- I'll never lose that weight
- I'll never be rich
- I can't dance/paint/sing/write/act...
- I'll never amount to anything

Some psychologists[9] believe the evolutionary purpose of this voice was to help protect us. I'm not sure about that, but after having talked with hundreds of people about this phenomenon, I know that it transcends age, gender, social status, nationality, and ethnicity. This Inner Critic is the primary reason why so many of us are paralyzed with self-doubt. How could we not be when every possible positive move, every step towards growth and exploration, is greeted with a nattering naysayer lodged right inside our head!

Some folks have told me that they know "who" this voice is. In many cases, it's the voice of an authority figure from our childhood. "Sister Mary Margaret," one 60ish woman related. "She always said I was a nobody." Another person told me that he heard the voice of his first grade teacher castigating him for dropping the chalk on the classroom floor.

Remember they taught it, you bought it? Sometimes we carry around hurtful things said to us in our childhood that impair us from living healthy adult lives. If we want to experience true freedom and gain access to our Inner Compass, we have to learn how to turn off the Inner Critic. Here are some exercises to do just that.

What to do now: Identify, release, and replace

Identify

In your journal write down anything you can think of whose source might be your Inner Critic. Just write and write and write—whatever

---

9   http://en.wikipedia.org/wiki/Inner_critic

comes to mind. "You smell, you're weak, you can't dance"...blah, blah, blah. Let the Inner Critic run for a bit and get it all on paper.

Now take a look at what you've written. Yuck! There's a bunch of unhelpful stuff. But don't worry - we are on a path to transformation. Now ask yourself, is there a person who might be associated with any or all of these statements?

If so, write down their names. If you can't remember their names, just put down something descriptive like, "third grade teacher", "little league coach", or "crossing guard".

Release

Now say out loud: "Sister Mary Margaret (or whomever), thank you for your help, but you are no longer needed. You are dismissed." Keep saying this to any person you may have identified. If you haven't identified anyone, just say, "My Inner Critic."

Replace

Now comes the fun part. This is where you get to pick your own all-star team to replace the Inner Critic. These are people—living, dead, historical, fictional...your choice—who you want to have access to any time you are faced with a challenge or need support. I have a colleague who calls this her Super Friends Group. The personal growth pioneer Napoleon Hill advocated creating just such an Inner Mastermind Group in his famous book *Think and Grow Rich*. You can also think of them as your Inner Dinner Party.

Just make a list of all the folks you want on your team. I've heard all kinds of fun ideas— from Oprah to Fred Flintstone to Harry Potter to Eleanor Roosevelt to Jesus, Buddha, and Walt Disney. The best part is that they can't turn you down. Remember, we are not asking people in real life to join our team; this is a completely internal project. You don't need to ask for their permission. Just close your eyes, welcome and thank them for joining your Dream Team. These folks are now on your side. They want the best for you and they have your back.

Last step

Take your "yuck" list of negative Inner Critic statements and tear it up into lots and lots of tiny pieces. My friend, the world-renowned intuitive En-May Mangels, suggests you tear up that yuck list into tiny pieces and burn them, flush them or bury them; we no longer want them to be part of your internal dialogue.

The next time you think about asking for that raise or consider buying that bathing suit or signing up for yodeling lessons, watch what happens. If your Inner Critic resurfaces, release it by saying: "Thanks for your help, but you are no longer needed. You are dismissed." Then summon up your Super Friends. Close your eyes for a second if you need to reconnect with them. Then ask them for their thoughts about the matter at hand. What a difference it makes to have an internal crew dedicated to supporting your best interests!

This is the first element in the Inner Compass Method. It's a big step towards overcoming self-doubt and building authentic self-confidence. But there's a lot more to come.

Important Note: If your Inner Critic is telling you that you should physically hurt yourself or others then something deeper may be going on and I urge you to seek professional help. Call 1-800-273-TALK (8255) and you'll be connected to a skilled, trained counselor at a crisis center in your area, anytime 24/7.

Chapter 4

Learning to Trust Yourself and
A Life or Death Decision

T urning off the Inner Critic and setting up your Dream Team are two important elements in learning to trust yourself. But before we go any further, I'd like to tell you a story.

It was a Tuesday, around 3:00 in the afternoon, when the phone rang.

It was my mom. She was hysterical.

"Your grandfather's just had a heart attack in the Seattle airport. He's on his way to Virginia Mason Hospital in an ambulance!"

At the time, I lived in Los Angeles and my 82 year old grandfather—the 6'2" patriarch of the family who had never been sick a day in his life—had come to Seattle to visit my cousin. Now he was in a coma. And so began a series of difficult decisions. Decisions that would mean the difference between life and death for a person who had been so very important to me.

Decision #1: Should I stay in Los Angeles or join the growing group of family members converging on the hospital? And what could I add to an already tense situation?

In order to make this decision, I did some soul-searching. In Buddhism we have a concept called "repaying debts of gratitude." I wondered if this could be an opportunity for me to repay him for all the ball games, birthday gifts, and penny poker nights that showed his love for me. My desire to try in some small way to "repay debts of gratitude" could, in hindsight, be seen as an example of a Noble Higher Purpose—which we'll talk more about later.

But I had just started a new job as head of development for a TV production company, so I had to beg my new boss for a few days off. Thankfully he agreed and I headed to Seattle.

When I arrived, the situation looked grim. Now two days into his coma, my grandfather was in the Intensive Care Unit with a respirator down his throat, and had started thrashing around. The once all-state football player was now an ashen, disheveled old man tied to a bed with tubes coming out every which way.

The doctor told us if he didn't come out of the coma soon, he might not make it. This, I learned, is called ICU syndrome—the longer you stay in the Intensive Care Unit, the less likely it is you'll ever get out.

Decision #2: After spending several hours with my grandfather, chanting my Buddhist mantra with no idea what to do, I recalled what a wise Buddhist friend had told me right before my departure: "If you're not willing to take 100% responsibility to resolve the situation, don't even bother going because you'll only make things worse."

You gotta love friends who give it to you straight!

From within welled up a powerful conviction. I looked at my co-matose grandfather and told him I would take 100% responsibility for his recovery.

The doctor didn't have an answer, my grandmother didn't have one, and the growing chorus of family members arriving at the hospital sure didn't either. So, I looked inside myself for an answer. I asked myself, "What would be the best thing for him?"

I suddenly realized that my grandfather was a fighter. He needed a chance to fight. This was a strong gut feeling—a deep internal knowing.

So I proposed my plan to grandma and she agreed. We summoned the doctor.

"Dial him off all the medication," I demanded. "We need to know if he's still there."

The doctor shook his head no. "You don't have the authority to do that."

"Who does?" I asked.

The doctor pointed to my grandmother. "It's risky," he told her.

But my grandmother was not to be trifled with. "Do what my grandson says," she replied.

Down the meds came and soon the thrashing stopped. I got right in his face and yelled at him, "Grandpa, if you can you hear me, nod your head yes." Slowly, he moved his head up and down. "Are you in pain?" He shook his head no. "Are you ready to fight?" He nodded again.

"Take out the respirator!" I ordered the doctor. He was stunned but complied.

My grandfather began breathing heavily. He needed to be off the respirator for an hour to prove he was strong enough to breathe on his own. Though he made a heroic effort, his heart rate shot up and he only lasted about a half hour before the doctor had the respirator reinserted.

A 6'2" all-state football player deserved the chance to fight for his life. And I knew that grandpa had to get off that respirator soon or the odds would quickly turn against him. So the next day we tried again and he lasted almost an hour. And by the third day—right after I had to leave to return to my new job (or my boss told me there might not be a job) – the respirator came out for good and he was moved out of Intensive Care. Less than a week later he had a triple bypass operation.

The old guy had plenty of life left in him and he went on to live for another 6 good years!

After he had recovered, I visited him at his home in Chicago. He leaned over and in his gruff voice said, "I don't know what you did back there in Seattle, but I want to thank you."

This is the power of making wise decisions and being able to trust yourself.

Over the years I have identified several life lessons that I learned from this profound experience:

- repaying debts of gratitude
- helping without an agenda other than the person's happiness
- seeking wise counsel
- not giving up in the face of adversity
- responding to unfolding events with flexibility
- balancing boldness with humility
- listening and trusting myself even if it goes against conventional wisdom

Each of these themes could be a whole book in and of themselves— and maybe I'll write about them in the future. For now, just take a moment and ask yourself this question: which of these do I regularly practice in my life?

Are you repaying debts of gratitude to others? Are you expressing gratitude? Who could you appreciate more? How about your spouse or partner, the sun, the moon, the trees or even the barista at Starbucks who makes your coffee?

When you help others, are you helping them do what you think is best for them or what they think is best for them? This is a key distinction. I spent many years helping people the way I thought they needed help, without bothering to ask them what help they really wanted or needed. What about you? Are you so tied up in your own agenda that you can't hear what others really need or want?

When you don't know the answer, are you willing to ask others for advice? Do you have anyone you trust enough in your life to seek wise counsel from? Even though this book is about trusting yourself first, I can assure you that I seek lots of wise counsel and expert advice before making decisions – because I want to make the most informed decision possible.

When things get tough, do you give up easily? I used to fold quickly as a kid when faced with problems. Then I became "tough" and was always looking for a fight. That didn't work so well either. Now, I'm more circumspect, but I will fight long and hard for what I believe in. What about you?

As events unfold, do you become paralyzed or energized? When in conflict with another person, do you find yourself digging in deeper, holding onto your position at all cost? Or are you able to respond to changing situations with flexibility? Once the daggers start flying, figuratively or literally, many people find themselves holding ever tighter to their positions. I vividly remember several heated arguments I had in my 20's where I found myself vigorously defending positions I wasn't sure I actually believed in; but damn it, I'd taken that position and I wasn't going to back down. This hasn't always turned out to be the best plan for me personally—in fact, I lost a few good friends and one great girlfriend that way. And it certainly hasn't turned out to be such a good plan in the history of leaders, companies, or nations.

Lastly, when facing a challenge or starting a new adventure, do you lean towards brashness or humility? Towards cowardice or boldness? The old saying reads, "Fortune favors the bold." In my own life I have found this to be true. But many times I've confused acting impetuously, recklessly or carelessly with boldness. And I can assure you, boldness at its best is none of those things.

Trusting yourself is about understanding who you are, how you tick and what you stand for. The more you know about yourself, the more that you like and respect yourself, the more you will be able to trust yourself.

Ultimately, the experience with my grandfather helped boost my confidence and my ability to trust myself. Now, you don't have to go through a life or death situation in order to develop this confidence. But if you should face such a crisis, emergency or other extreme situation, I want you to be able to trust your ability to make the right decisions in the moment—something we'll talk more about later.

First, we need to start laying the foundation of self-trust. And it starts with a simple exercise.

Start by loving yourself first. I have heard many stories of people who simply repeated the phrase "I love myself, I love myself, I love myself" over and over as if it was a mantra. I've co-facilitated groups using the Emotional Freedom Technique (EFT) where this phrase was used in conjunction with tapping on energy meridians along the surface of the body. The results on individuals in these groups were striking. And I heartily recommend a wonderful short book written by Kamal Ravikant, entitled *Love Yourself Like Your Life Depends On It*. Kamal tells how he moved from being defeated, dejected and depressed to functional, hopeful and reinvigorated, all through integrating this single phrase into his consciousness on a daily basis.

I have tried it myself, and it works. It is elegantly simple, yet profound. Think of this as a new way to get yourself out of a funk, to get centered, or even just to relax before bed.

What to do now: Spend some time loving yourself

Spend the next 5 minutes repeating to yourself out loud the following three words:

I love myself.

Set a timer and begin. Watch carefully to see if the Inner Critic surfaces. If it shows up just say, "Thanks for your help, but you are no longer needed. You are dismissed." Then summon up your Super Friends and keep repeating, "I love myself."

Feel free to go on longer than five minutes. Keep repeating until you either fall into a blissful sleep or feel something shift.

Extra credit

Take out your journal and write down the following phrase:

"If I truly loved myself I would..." then fill in the blank.

Now write the phrase: "If I truly loved myself I would..." again, and fill in the blank with a different response.

Keep going until you've written at least six sentences. And if you are moved to keep going, keep writing until you run out of responses.

Which of these actions, if taken starting today, would transform your life for the better?

What will be your first small step today in this direction?

Chapter 5

Noble Higher Purpose

L earning how to trust yourself means being able to make wise and effective decisions about any important issue or question in your life. While we can seek wise counsel from people whose opinions we might respect, we don't want to be reliant on others for deciding the course of our lives. Nor do we want to be constantly second guessing ourselves once we do make a decision. We need to be able to evaluate our options, determine the best course for our highest good, make a clear decision, and then move forward with confidence. This is what the Inner Compass Method is all about.

When I teach decision making to business people and students, we spend a lot of time talking about logical, rational and analytical methods for considering important decisions. We work on identifying and expanding our options, doing research and analysis, etc. This is all very valuable and I highly recommend a systematic approach to making decisions. In fact you can learn my entire decision-making process using the Inner Compass Method via an excellent online course[10] I've created.

As valuable as all the logical, rational and analytical stuff is for decision-making, it won't really help you learn how to trust yourself. The key to the ending self-doubt is identifying what I call a Noble

---

10   http://modernwisdom.com/stress-free-decision-making-s1/

Higher Purpose. A Noble Higher Purpose is a way of asking, "What is the deeper meaning behind my need to make this decision?"

A Noble Higher Purpose is a statement that expresses something of benefit for me and something of benefit or service to others—whether it be for my wife, my customers, the nation, the whales, the planet, etc. If it's only about me it can quickly fall into egotism. And if my Noble Higher Purpose is only about others, but has nothing of benefit for me, it can become too removed from my reality. We need something that has the marriage of benefit for both ourselves and others.

Why do we need to do this? Because when we can identify a Noble Higher Purpose for each decision we are facing, we automatically elevate our level of consciousness. As a result, a new kind of intelligence opens up for us, and our ability to tap into our inner wisdom increases. After working with hundreds of people, I have also come to believe that when we can frame our decision question around benefit to ourselves and service to others, the whole universe starts working in sync with us to help solve our problem.

So what are some examples of a Noble Higher Purpose statement? The most basic one I use with students and clients is:

- For my highest good and in the greatest service of others...

Then you can add more specific statements as well, such as:

- To create financial independence while serving at least 50 clients a year
- To find the best living situation for my mom while uniting with my siblings
- To live in harmony with my husband and be able to pursue my dream of writing
- To double our income and still have time and energy for our children and hobbies
- To cure my illness completely and encourage others with my survival story

Remember the story about my grandfather's heart attack? Well, in hindsight, I could have used this Noble Higher Purpose to guide my decision-making: "To repay my debt of gratitude to my grandfather".

The one I use when making decisions for my company Modern Wisdom is, "To build a company that provides me with financial freedom and helps millions of people around the world live more joyful and fulfilling lives."

Even a seemingly mundane decision can have a Noble Higher Purpose. Let's say you need to choose between buying the blue Prius and the silver Honda. A Noble Higher Purpose statement might be something like, "To find reliable transportation so I can get to work on time, provide for my family and contribute to society".

This is an important idea. In his book *Drive*, Daniel Pink analyzes four decades of human motivation science. Pink explains, "Humans, by their nature, seek purpose – a cause greater and more enduring than themselves." In other words, having a Noble Higher Purpose connects you to a greater wisdom or intelligence that only comes when you are in service to others.

But I think Lisa McLeod, who teaches about purpose-driven sales systems, put it best: "Purpose ignites the secret yearnings of our hearts". Based on her research, she found that purpose-driven sales-people outperform product-driven salespeople. She says, "Purpose may sound fluffy, but it translates into cold hard cash".

I know this to be true from my work as a business strategy adviser. I help businesses of all sizes find what I call their "Big P Purpose". Doing so creates a dynamic change that can galvanize an entire company.

Psychologists tell us that human beings have two fundamental emotional needs: we want connection and we want meaning. We want to have close personal relationships and we want our work to count for something. We all want to make a difference.

What to do now: Write it down

Every year you will make thousands of decisions. Some of these, like the story I shared earlier about my grandfather's heart attack, will be life-changing for you, your loved ones, co-workers, clients and customers.

Take a moment to write down any issue, problem or decision you're facing right now in your life. Writing it down has power; it takes the issue out of your head and puts it right in front of you.

Again, this could be a personal issue, a business problem, something relating to family, relationships, finance, health, or whatever is troubling you most right now. Let's work on it together.

While I'm sure you really want to get an answer to your life's most pressing questions, I would like to suggest that you start off with a relatively small problem or question before tackling any big hairy life-changing decisions. Once you get the hang of the Inner Compass Method, those emotionally charged decisions will become easier to answer.

Next, write down a Noble Higher Purpose statement that is underlying your decision. Don't worry about grammar or perfect sentence structure; just write down your hoped-for personal benefit and the intended benefit for the other people involved.

For example, if your decision is about a career choice, your Noble Higher Purpose statement might be something like, "To create financial independence while serving at least 50 clients a year."

Or if your decision question is about how to settle a problem between you and your spouse, your Noble Higher Purpose statement might be something like, "For my highest good and for our greatest family harmony."

Whatever works for you is OK as long as it includes something of benefit for you and something of benefit or service to others.

Now that we have a decision to experiment with and a Noble Higher Purpose statement, we can get into the nitty gritty of learning how to trust yourself using the Inner Compass Method.

✦

Chapter 6

Introduction to the
Inner Compass Method

N ow comes the fun part of learning to trust yourself.

Remember when we talked earlier about inner wisdom? This is the part of you that always has your best interests in mind. It is your highest self, your enlightened self and the part of you that wants you to succeed. In fact, its whole purpose is to help you become happy, successful and fulfilled. It's standing by 24/7, waiting to help you. But you have to know how to access it.

The way to access this wonderful part of our lives is by using a process I call the Inner Compass Method. By asking specific questions in a specific manner, using a Noble Higher Purpose statement, anyone can gain access to their highest self. A wise person once said that the answers are all lying around waiting for us to think up the right questions. With the right questions and the right technique, you too can get answers.

You may find this easy to do or it might take a few tries, but I can assure you that after working with hundreds of people, anyone and everyone has the ability to access their Inner Compass—including you. Thankfully, the work you've already done in this book has helped pave the way.

However, there is one condition: our Inner Compass must be used for our greatest good and the greatest good of others. It can't be used to hurt anyone, manipulate people, pick ponies, play the stock market, or predict the future—so don't go there. Trust me.

Here are some examples of decisions made by my clients and students using the Inner Compass Method you are about to learn.

My accountant, Sue, wanted to know when to retire. She was over 60, her husband had already retired and they wanted to travel together. But Sue had been working for over 25 years, and was devoted to her clients. She just couldn't imagine saying goodbye to all of them—many of whom had become like family to her. Then I taught her the Inner Compass Method and she got her answer. Six months later, there I was at her retirement party. When asked to say a few words, she thanked everyone, pointed at me, and said it was all my fault! There was a loud chorus of light-hearted booing in my direction. But Sue quickly confirmed that retiring now, while she and her husband were still in good health, was the best decision she could have ever made.

A tester of an early version of the Inner Compass Method was my wife's close friend. An attractive, vivacious and talented technology executive, she had been in a relationship with a man for over 10 years. They lived together and co-owned property, but the magic was gone. She could see all the reasons for staying in the relationship—stability, familiarity, comfort—but wondered if there was something better for her.

I taught her the Inner Compass Method and as we got deeper into the process, the tears started to flow. Her Inner Compass confirmed what her heart had been trying to tell her—the relationship was over and it was time to move on. Now she is enjoying an active social life, traveling and rediscovering her passions.

Another client was the President of a major trade council. Originally we had planned to work together on a personnel issue in her organization. But when I asked her to pick the top problem which, if solved today, would have the most beneficial impact on her life, she chose to tackle a family situation. She revealed that her daughter had become addicted to heroin. As her daughter's addiction grew, she became abusive and started stealing from her parents. Now, after being kicked out of rehab, she was living with her drug dealer boyfriend, and was begging her mother to allow her to move back home.

My client and her husband agonized over this situation for weeks. Knowing their only daughter was living in a drug house was truly painful, but they knew what had happened the last time they allowed her back home. Using the Inner Compass Method, she found the answer: allow her daughter to come home, but set clear boundaries for her. If the daughter crossed the line, she would be kicked out again. My client spoke to her daughter's counselor and doctor, and with clear rules established, her daughter came home.

On another occasion, my own daughter called me about a friend who was in crisis. This friend had gotten a full scholarship to the Massachusetts Institute of Technology, but she was miserable and wanted to drop out and move home. I set up a Skype session with her and she picked up the Inner Compass Method very quickly. Because she was so distraught, we asked a very specific and time-sensitive question: "For my highest good and in the greatest service to others, should I leave MIT today?"

Now, I never try to impose my own opinions or prejudices on the people I'm working with, but I have to tell you I was relieved to hear that the answer was "No." The next question was, "For my highest good and in the greatest service of others, do I have a mission to fulfill at MIT?" And the answer was "Yes." Now we were starting to get somewhere. I then had her make a list of her passions and skills and rate them. After doing so, we were able to use her Inner Compass to identify which of these passions was part of her mission at MIT. This specific process later evolved into a program I now call Finding Your Life Direction with the Inner Compass Method, which has helped numerous people determine the right path for their lives. Today she is a thriving part of the MIT community.

This young woman also happens to be a big Harry Potter fan. And after experiencing the Inner Compass Method she said, "Marc what you are doing is teaching magic to muggles!" What a great metaphor.

It is immensely gratifying to see people who have been wracked with self-doubt, paralyzed by fear, or stuck in denial find real clarity. But not all of my Inner Compass Method stories are this heavy. As you'll see later on, people can use this method for fun or even mundane questions. No matter how you use it, this process can be of great help in learning to trust yourself.

The easiest way to access your Inner Compass is by bringing an open mind and an open heart. So let's play with this. I've got some very simple physical exercises that I've found useful for getting out of my head and allowing myself to get more in touch with my body and my intuition that you may find helpful.

Grounding and Centering Exercises

Let's start by getting grounded. We'll use three simple exercises to do some right brain/left brain linking and grounding. This will also help quiet the mind and turn down the everyday chatter in our heads. I learned these techniques from my friend, the "Energy Queen" She-evaun Moran.

Figure 2. Head Cradle

Head Cradle: Take the index and middle finger of your left hand and place them on your upper lip just under your nose. Now take your right hand and gently cradle the base of your skull; use your thumb to lightly massage the upper part of your neck. Breathe in deeply and release. Repeat for several deep breaths. Place your hands in your lap when finished.

Cross Arm Earlobe Massage: Take your left hand and cross it over your chest

Figure 3. Cross Arm Earlobe Massage

Figure 4. Crossed Ankles, Crossed Wrists

Figure 5. Deep Centering Breathing

to gently grab your right earlobe with your thumb and index finger. Now take your right hand and grab your left earlobe. You'll find your arms crossed over your chest. Gently massage both earlobes as you breathe in deeply. Feel free to close your eyes and let your head drop as you do this. Take several deep breaths and release. This one is great for getting out of your head and quieting your thoughts. But don't try this one while driving! Place your hands back in your lap when finished.

Crossed Ankles, Crossed Wrists: Cross your left ankle lightly over your right ankle. Now take your right wrist and cross it over your left wrist. Breathe deeply and release. This is one you can do in a meeting or class if you get antsy or distracted. Uncross your legs and arm and rest your hands back in your lap when finished.

Deep Centering Breathing: Place your feet flat on the floor. Place both hands resting in your lap, with your thumbs around your navel. Why here? Chinese traditional medicine tells us there is a point about two inches below the navel called the lower dan tien which acts like the spiritual radiator of the body. Close your eyes. Touch the tip of your tongue to the roof of your mouth. Sit up straight, head centered – neither falling forward or back. While your eyes are closed, try looking up slightly under your closed eyelids.

Now take three deep, relaxing breaths. Breathe in for 6 counts, hold for 3 counts, and exhale for 6 counts. Pause and hold at the bottom of the exhale for 3 counts.

Now breathe in and repeat this through three breath cycles.

You should find yourself more present, relaxed and aware after these grounding and centering exercises. If not, feel free to do all or part of the exercises again until you feel centered and grounded.

To watch a short video of these grounding exercises, see the link in footnote 11 below.[11]

Here we go!

We are now going to ask our body, our Inner Compass, to show us what the answer "yes" to a question would look or feel like in our body. It might be a tug, a twitch or a pull to one side, or a feeling of motion—either forward or back, or even a head shake like a horse. It might be a picture or a symbol, a flash or a color. Everyone is different, and everyone can do this. You don't even have to think about it—it will just come to you.

Let's try this together.

1. Place your feet flat on the floor, neck relaxed, shoulders relaxed, hands resting around your navel, tongue on the roof of your mouth, looking up slightly in closed eyelids.
2. Take a nice deep breath in, and blow it out.
3. Ask yourself out loud: "For my highest good and in the greatest service of others, please show me what the answer "yes" looks or feels like in my body."

Remember, we aren't forcing anything. We're just allowing our Inner Compass to surface. Whatever comes up is what we'll work with.

Did you get something? It might be very subtle or it could be strong. Everyone's experience is unique.

Now let's find your "no" signal or symbol.

---

11   http://youtu.be/40PlFiNHjnE

1. Place your feet flat on the floor, neck relaxed, shoulders relaxed, hands resting around your navel, tongue on the roof of your mouth, looking up slightly in closed eyelids.
2. Take a nice deep breath in, and blow it out.
3. Ask yourself out loud: "For my highest good and in the greatest service of others, please show me what the answer "no" looks or feels like in my body."

Test Questions

Now let's test it. We're going to ask some yes/no questions.

Ask yourself out loud: "For my highest good, and in the greatest service of others, is my name [state your name]?"

What did you get? This should be your "yes" signal or symbol.

Now try this one: "For my highest good, and in the greatest service of others, is my name Millard Fillmore?"

What did you get this time? This should be your "no" signal or symbol.

Here's another test question: "For my highest good, and in the greatest service of others, do I live at [state your current address]."

Now try this one: "For my highest good and in the greatest service of others, do I live at 1600 Pennsylvania, Avenue Washington, DC?"

You should get your "no" answer or signal to that last one – if not, you are the President of the United States!

These questions are aimed at helping you get a sense of your "yes" and "no" signals from your Inner Compass. There is no right or wrong answer. Some people just feel a tug or pull of their head in one direction for "yes" and the opposite for "no." Others see images, like my friend who loves lighthouses: her "yes" symbol was the image of a sweeping bright light from a lighthouse. Another saw her favorite pet from childhood. Others have only feelings without images. Whatever works for you is OK. Our goal is to achieve consistency so you can begin to trust your Inner Compass signal.

More Information Needed

OK, one last piece. We have been asking yes/no questions, but sometimes we need a third option: "more information needed". This might indicate that we didn't ask the right question or there's more to evaluate before we can get a clear answer.

Let's expand our Inner Compass and test for that as well. OK?

Eyes closed, looking up slightly in your closed eyelids, tongue on the roof of your mouth. Shoulders relaxed. Feet flat on the floor. Please say out loud: "For my highest good and in the greatest service of others, please show me what the answer 'more information needed' looks or feels like in my body."

Write down what you get. I have a friend who told me he saw the image of a traffic signal. Red meant "no," green meant "yes" and the yellow light meant "more info needed."

Keep working with your "yes," "no" and "more information needed" signals until you become comfortable with this process. If you feel like you need some extra help, I have created a guided video[12] of the process with my friend and colleague En-May Mangels.

---

12 http://youtu.be/S_7qL6X3UqI

Chapter 7

Testing Options Using Your Inner Compass

N ow let's tie it all together.

Look back to the exercise, "What to do now: Write it down" (page 42), where you chose a specific problem or decision you are facing right now in your life. Now write down several possible options that might solve your problem or answer your question. These can range from the obvious and logical to the creative or even improbable. Don't let your Inner Critic get in the way here; we want to let the ideas flow.

Let's take a look at the Noble Higher Purpose statement you wrote down for your decision. We'll be using this statement to power up our Inner Compass. Pick the first option that you'd like to test.

For example, "For my highest good and in the greatest service of others and in line with my Noble Higher Purpose of doubling our income and still having time for our children and hobbies, is working from home the best option for me at this time?"

Now it's your turn.

Place your feet flat on the floor with your hands resting comfortably near your navel. Let your tongue touch the roof of your mouth, and look up slightly with your eyelids closed. Take a nice deep breath in, and blow it out slowly. Use the handy formula below for crafting your question:

"For my highest good and in the greatest service of others
and in line with my Noble Higher Purpose

of _____

[state your Noble Higher Purpose]

is _____

[state an option]

the best option for me now?"

Figure 6. Formula For Using Your Inner Compass

You should be looking for your "yes," "no," or "more info needed" signal or symbol.

What response did you get? Are you surprised? Write it down.

If you got your "more info needed" signal or symbol, that means you may have to do some more homework on that option or refine the way you stated your question.

Let's test another option.

Place your feet flat on the floor with your hands resting comfortably near your navel. Let your tongue touch the roof of your mouth, and look up slightly with your eyelids closed. Take a nice deep breath in, and blow it out slowly. Use the formula in Figure 6. to test your next option.

If you have more options that you'd like to test, you can repeat this section as many times as you'd like until you get clarity. The more you practice this technique, the better you'll become at accessing your Inner Compass.

I recommend that you try this sitting upright or even standing up, balancing lightly on the balls of your feet. Sometimes your Inner Compass signal may be so subtle that if you are lying down or leaning back in a chair you may not feel it.

By working regularly with your Inner Compass you will begin to build confidence in your ability to make wise and effective decisions.

And because you are always framing each question with a Noble Higher Purpose statement, you cannot in any way harm yourself or others using this process.

If your Inner Critic pops up during the process, you know what to say: "Thanks for your help, but you are no longer needed. You are dismissed." Then summon up your Super Friends group. Close your eyes for a second if you need to reconnect with them and then continue with the Inner Compass Method process.

Once you have opened the door to your Inner Compass, you will discover a whole new world of possibilities. There's so much you can do using your Inner Compass to improve the quality of your life and the world around you, but we'll get into that a little later on.

Tips for Successfully Working with Your Inner Compass

As you experiment with your Inner Compass, notice if anything changes over time. Has your emotional state settled, become more peaceful or calm? If your emotional state has gotten more intense or if you feel upset, please take a break; drink some water and rest before continuing. Our goal is to make decisions and get answers that bring clarity, relief, and even excitement, but never suffering.

If you get your "more information needed" signal more than once while testing your options, ask yourself if you are stating the question properly. You can also ask if you have the best Noble Higher Purpose for the decision. It's perfectly OK to go back and revise your decision question or Noble Higher Purpose. It sometimes takes more than one try to get a Nobel Higher Purpose statement that really allows your Inner Compass to kick in. If you still have questions, see the Frequently Asked Questions section at the end of the book.

If you get an answer using the Inner Compass Method that surprises or confuses you, try asking yourself: "If I did not have any limitation of time, money or fear, would I make the same decision?" Consider that time, money and especially fear are often just constructs we have created and can be overcome with determination and creativity. For more on this, I recommend the book *Feel The Fear and Do It Anyway* by Susan Jeffers.

Chapter 8

An Encounter with the Buddhist Yoda, Part 2

R emember the story I told at the beginning of this book, about how I struggled with horrible migraines, stomach pains, and nasty digestion problems until the Buddhist Yoda recommended I ask my food if I should eat it? Well, what about you? Do you have any nagging health issues? How about trouble sleeping, irritable bowels, coughing spells, heart palpitations, bladder problems, or mysterious aches and pains? Sinus congestion, post nasal drip, or weird stuff in your ears?

Look, I would never tell you to ignore the advice of trained medical professionals. But with shorter and shorter doctor's office appointments and lots of pressure on doctors to do all kinds of unnecessary tests, you may want to get a second opinion—your own!

Try these simple Inner Compass exercises and embrace your inner diagnostician.

What to do now: Discover your good food/bad food

Lets' start with a simple version of the method I used in the story above. Go into your kitchen, grab any item from your pantry or refrigerator and hold it against your abdomen—your gut. Take a nice deep breath in and exhale. Now say out loud, "For my highest good and for my greatest health, should I eat/drink this?"

What answer did you get? Write it down. Pick another item and try again. Test this experiment on 5-6 items.

Were you surprised at some of the results?

Your body has wisdom. It knows what is best for it. The more you practice this experiment, the stronger the response you'll be able to receive from your body.

Many years ago I went through my kitchen and discovered there were lots of things I had been eating for years—foods I loved—that were "reading" or testing badly for my body. So I eliminated them. Some things I quit cold turkey, like wheat and dairy. Others have been harder to remove from my diet, like processed sugar—something I still wrestle with. I stopped taking aspirin and Tylenol until my digestive system could restore itself. I stopped drinking beer—and I loved beer! And I stopped drinking coffee— and I loved coffee! But my health came first.

Today I am much healthier than I was in my late 20s. Sure, I weigh a few more pounds, but I have been good to myself for a very long time. And if I now want to have the occasional slice of pizza—formerly a quick ticket to a hellish sinus headache—I can. But I understand that my body just doesn't like wheat, dairy and heavily processed meats like pepperoni, so I don't often indulge.

Once you've tried the experiment above you can move on to the next one.

What to do now: What's up, doc?

Write down every ache, pain, and nagging or chronic health problem you are facing right now. Be honest, none of us has perfect health all the time. And if you've been coping—I hate the term coping —with ongoing health problems, why not ask your higher self, your inner wisdom, for some help.

Pick the problem or issue that is most challenging or vexing to you. Maybe you have cancer, or high blood pressure. Maybe you're taking a wild mixture of medications. Pick one of your medications and set it on the table in front of you.

Close your eyes and imagine a compass face - with markings indicating north, south, east and west. Now let's assign each direction a characteristic we'd like to test. For now, west means the item we are testing is strengthening. East means the item we are testing is weakening. And north means the item is neutral. Envision a pointer resting at the southern mark.

Now, take the medication you'd like to test in both hands and hold it against your gut or abdomen. Close your eyes, envision the compass face, and say out loud, "For my highest good and for my greatest health, is this medication having a strengthening, neutral or weakening effect on me?"

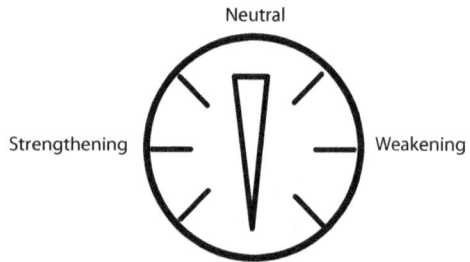

Figure 7. Testing Compass

Then just allow the pointer to go where it will. It should settle on one of the compass points soon. No need to force it. We are just allowing our inner wisdom to take over. If the pointer lands on south, this could mean "more information needed."

What did you discover? Did you get a clear read on that medication? If not, try again. If you did get a clear reading, then move on and try some of the other medications in your cabinet.

What is all this telling you about your health and the medicines, beverages, and foods you are ingesting daily?

* **Important Note**: I do not recommend stopping any prescription medication without consulting your doctor. Even if you get a strong "weakening" reading from a medication, I do not suggest you stop taking it cold turkey. Doing so could have an unexpected and danger-ous impact on your health. I would suggest you call your doctor and tell him or her that you'd like to discuss reducing or getting off the medication in question. If your physician is open to this conversation, then you may be able to come up with a plan together. If your physi-cian is not open to this, then it might be time to consider finding a new medical provider.

Chapter 9

Navigating Through Daily Life with the Inner Compass

N ow that you are starting to get the hang of the Inner Compass Method, we can begin exploring a whole new universe of potential applications for this knowledge. The more you practice, the more uses you'll find for your Inner Compass in your daily life. The following are a few of my favorites.

Eating out

We've already seen that you can use your Inner Compass to determine what foods and medications in your house are best for you. Why not take this skill out into the world.

Here's a simple exercise you can do that will not only help you strengthen your Inner Compass but can also make dining out more fun. It might even save you from a nasty illness.

Let's say you are going out to dinner at a restaurant. Once inside the restaurant, you can use your Inner Compass to pick which item on the menu would be best for your health and enjoyment.

While most restaurants make efforts to share ingredient information with diners, many of them use all kinds of preservatives, flavor enhancers, sweeteners and thickeners that don't show up on the menu.

If you like Asian food, for example, be prepared for MSG sneaking into your favorite dishes. Even if the server tells you they don't add MSG, it may be an ingredient in the pre-prepared sauces and mixes that are used in the kitchen. As much as I love Japanese, Chinese, Thai, and Korean food, I am sensitive to MSG and often got nasty headaches after what seemed like perfectly healthy meals.

Fortunately, we have our Inner Compass. Of course, if I'm out to dinner at a restaurant, it wouldn't be appropriate for me to do a bunch of breathing and grounding exercises at my table—especially if I'm eating with my wife or business colleagues. So instead, I access my Inner Compass using a shorter version of the process.

I simply put my index finger over an item on the menu that looks good and then I touch my chest where my heart is located. Silently I ask myself, "For my highest good and for my greatest health, should I order this item?" And then I get my answer.

Since I've been doing this a long time, I can access my Inner Compass with my eyes open. You may have to briefly shut your eyes to get a clear signal or sign. You may also find that to get a strong reading or signal you need to say this phrase out loud.

More and more Americans are eating meals outside of the home, either because of convenience, time limitations, or culinary preferences. But not all food is created equal, and being able to choose the right food for your best health can be extremely beneficial.

Here's another reason why you might want to take this seriously. I've been using this method for more than 15 years and in that time I have never contracted food poisoning. I've traveled through the Orient, South America, Mexico, and Europe. Could it be that my Inner Compass is steering me away from foods and beverages that could make me really sick?

What to do now: What's on the menu

Take yourself out to lunch or dinner at a local restaurant. When the menu comes, look it over like you would normally and find a dish that seems appealing.

Place your feet flat on the floor. Use your right index finger to touch the listing of the dish you are considering and place your left hand over your heart. If you feel comfortable, close your eyes, and then ask yourself silently, "For my highest good and my greatest health, should I order this?"

Be alert for a more subtle version of your "yes," "no" or "more info needed" signal. Have confidence that your inner wisdom wants you to eat just as well when you are at a restaurant as when you are at home.

If you get your "no" signal, don't be discouraged. Find another dish and ask again. Sometimes you may find that there aren't choices on the menu from which you can get a strong "yes" answer. Here's where you can be creative. Try substituting an ingredient.

Knowing that I'm better off when I avoid wheat and dairy, I will sometimes ask to modify a menu item that looks promising. For example, I might ask my Inner Compass, "For my highest good and my greatest health, should I order the chicken breast, but without the Monterrey Jack cheese?"

Keep working until you get a good strong signal from your Inner Compass.

You can take it up a notch by comparing one menu item with another. For example, let's say I'm debating between the Garlic Chicken and the Ginger Tofu lunch special at my favorite Thai Restaurant. I take one of my index fingers and place it over the listing for the Garlic Chicken and place my other index finger on the Ginger Tofu listing. Then I ask myself, "For my highest good and my greatest health, which of these items should I order?" I'm looking for a pull, a tug or a feeling of being drawn to one of these two choices.

If I get my "more info needed" signal, I know I probably shouldn't order either of them and I start over with some new choices.

Entertainment

It might sound like a trivial use of one's inner wisdom, but the truth is that your time is precious and you really don't want to waste two hours – and $20 – on a bad movie. It doesn't matter what your definition of a good or bad movie is—you may love Iron Man and hate Shakespeare, that's fine. The point is to be able to quickly identify movies that you would enjoy based on your taste.

What to do now: On the big screen

Take out the movie section of your local paper. Find a film you wouldn't normally pick and try asking your Inner Compass about it.

Place your feet flat on the floor. Place your right index finger on the choice you are considering and place your left hand over your heart. If you feel comfortable, close your eyes and ask yourself out loud, "For my highest good, in the greatest service of others, and for my greatest enjoyment, should I go see this movie?"

What was the answer? Did it surprise you? You might just discover a whole new genre of films.

You can do the same thing with TV shows, plays, and even books. When I'm browsing for books at my local bookstore and I find a title that looks interesting, sometimes I'll just buy it. But if I'm on the fence— maybe it's 500 pages and I'm not sure I really want to make that kind of time commitment— then I'll take the book to a quiet corner of the store and ask myself, "For my highest good, and in the greatest service to others, should I buy this book?" If I get a yes, I know I'll be lugging it along with me for a good while until I get through it.

Once while testing a book in a bookstore, I kept getting my "no" signal accompanied by a quick swoosh to my "more info needed" sign.

I couldn't figure out what my Inner Compass was trying to tell me. So I started asking more detailed questions.

"Would I enjoy reading this book?" Answer: "yes."

"Should I buy this book now?" Answer: "no."

"Should I buy this book some other time?" Answer: "no."

"Should I buy this book on Amazon.com?" Answer: "no."

I started to get frustrated. My Inner Compass was telling me that I'd like the book, but I kept getting seemingly contradictory answers. Finally I asked, "For my highest good and in the greatest service to others, should I read this book but not buy it?'

Suddenly, I got a very strong "yes" answer. Then it dawned on me, the book I was holding in my hands was expensive and at the time cash was scarce in our house. So I asked, "Can I find this book in the library?" Answer: "YES!"

Duh! I then quickly scanned the local libraries with my Inner Compass. "Can this book be found at my local library?" "Yes!" Two days later on a rainy afternoon, I was in a cozy chair at my local library enjoying my new read.

These are just two examples of ways you can use your Inner Compass to help you save time and money, and enjoy your life more. Remember, this ability is inherent in all people and is on call 24/7 to assist you. Once you start using your Inner Compass you'll find even more ways to apply this amazing tool.

Chapter 10

Big Decisions, Thorny Dilemmas, and Tough Choices

"NO CLEAR SOLUTION IN MIDDLE EAST CRISIS"
"VOTERS SAY NO GOOD CHOICES IN STATE ELECTION"
"HOUSE SPEAKER OUT OF OPTIONS"

These are just some of the headlines I've read recently that illustrate the idea that many conflicts or crises have no good solutions. My clients often come to me with problems for which they believe there are only bad options. For example: fire someone or be fired; ignore an embezzler or confront them and expose the company as inept; care for an aging parent with Alzheimer's in your own home or send them to an assisted living program; throw out your drug addicted son or let him keep stealing from you to supply his habit.

None of these are easy choices, I know. Two of the examples above are from my own life.

So, how should we deal with these situations?

The correct term for this kind of thorny problem is a dilemma. The definition of a dilemma is: "A choice between two or more options, none of which is attractive."[13] A tragic example from contemporary fiction would be the novel *Sophie's Choice*, where the lead character

---

13   Citation: Webster's Dictionary

must choose which of her two children will go with her to a Nazi labor camp and which will go right to the gas chambers.

So what do we do when we are faced with two or more bad choices? It's one thing if we don't really have to make a decision, or even if we can put off making a choice and wait to see if better options show up over time. But when we are under the gun, so to speak, it can be easy to fall into despair or be paralyzed with doubt.

These are often moral or ethical dilemmas. I learned this firsthand when I was right out of college working as a waiter in a downtown Chicago restaurant. I was on the subway going home, in the early hours of Sunday morning, when I saw a man passed out drunk on a seat in the middle of the subway car. Another man came up behind him and began going through the passed out guy's pockets. Not a soul on the train made a move to stop him. I began to rise out of my seat and as I did the robber flashed the handle of a knife. I meekly sat back down. The robber finished his work and quickly exited the train. No one made any effort to follow him. When I got off at the end of the line, the guy was still passed out on the seat, now light his wallet, watch, and who knows what else.

That was a turning point for me. Talk about self-doubt— I couldn't sleep the whole night long. How should I have responded? What if it had been me passed out? The more I wrestled with these questions, the more I concluded that there were no good options. Defend the guy and face the knife. Cave and be judged a coward in the court of my own conscience.

I resolved to find a way to discern the correct choice for any such situation. Over the past 20 years, I have compiled a mental checklist.

The first step is to make sure I'm not facing a false dilemma. In other words, could there be more choices available to me than the obvious but unattractive ones I've already identified? In the subway car, for example, what else could I have done? In retrospect, I could have found the train conductor and told him about the robbery, called the police, or even just yelled at the robber to stop. There were, in fact, a multitude of other options that I hadn't considered.

The second step is what I call "future projecting." I learned this simple strategy for double-checking decisions from *O Magazine* contributor Suzy Welch. In her book *10-10-10* she suggests readers ask themselves three questions when making any big decision:

- What will the consequences of my decision be in 10 minutes?
- What about in 10 months?
- And in 10 years?

Suzy says the answers not only help her make the best decision possible, but also explain her choices to the family members, friends or coworkers who might be impacted by said decision.

She has used the 10-10-10 strategy to make some of her most meaningful decisions, including her divorce. I have also found that this can be a simple method for determining which of two (or more) unattractive options might actually be the right choice in a difficult situation.

But now you have an even better tool. When things seem most unclear, when the problem seems to border on impossible, it's time to turn to your Inner Compass to help you achieve clarity. Had I known about the Inner Compass Method when I was riding that subway car in my youth, I could have called it up on the spot and gotten an answer that was in my highest good and the highest good of the person being robbed. It is impossible for me to know all these years later what that answer might have been, but I'm confident that should I find myself in a similar situation now, I'd be able to find the right answer within myself.

Now that you've learned the Inner Compass Method, you'll not only be able to handle the toughest decisions in your life, you'll also be able to discern the truth of what others are saying and doing in your environment.

Chapter 11

Trusting Others—Keys to Building Real Trust

As we discussed earlier in this book, in order to trust others we first have to learn how to trust ourselves. You've now made a number of powerful steps in that direction and I hope you are enjoying the benefits of renewed self-confidence and clarity.

However, no man or woman is an island, and in our increasingly interconnected and interdependent world, we are forced to interact with dozens, if not hundreds, of people a day. So how do you know who is trustworthy?

One way of determining if someone is telling the truth or not is by using a lie detector test.

Yes, a lie detector.

What if I told you that you already possess the most accurate, foolproof lie detector ever created right inside of your life? It is accessible to you at all hours of the day or night and it is never, I repeat, never wrong.

Some of you might be tempted to shut this book or switch off your tablet, thinking, "I really liked what this guy Marc was sharing, but this lie detector stuff is just too crazy!"

Stay with me.

Many cultures have shorthand for seeking information about whether a person is telling the truth. In some places, a person's word is their bond, and if they are caught lying or cheating they become an outcast. In certain ancient cultures, promises were only considered valid if made while looking into each others' eyes because the eyes were considered the windows to the soul. But in our society, people lie all the time and sometimes they'll even look you in the eye while doing it!

So how can we really know if the car dealership is telling the truth about the "barely used" Honda you are thinking of buying or whether the investment opportunity you've just been offered is too good to be true? How can you know whether the politician seeking your vote is on the level or has already sold out to some big money interests?

Your Inner Compass can help you.

Let me tell you a story...

When I worked in television, I was fortunate enough to help sell a ten-hour series to Time Warner called "The History of Rock 'N Roll." This excellent series still airs on cable TV and featured over 200 interviews with some of the top movers, shakers and rockers in the music industry. As supervising producer I had to hire a lot of people—and quickly. Big name documentary producers, celebrity wannabe directors and all kinds of people began flooding my mailbox and voicemail with pitches to fill the coveted 10 slots for this series. I had to make recommendations to my boss, Time Warner, and Quincy Jones—who was the executive producer. Careers would be launched or enhanced based on the decisions I made. And people in Hollywood have long memories, especially when they feel they've been "dissed" or slighted in some way.

I made the choices as best I could and most of them were accepted. But the true challenge came from a completely unexpected place. One day, well into the production, my boss informed me that I was now responsible for the show's music supervisor. This person was in charge of licensing the rights for all the songs that would be played throughout the series. It was a complex gig with lots of potential problems with musicians, unions, music publishers, record labels, and TV networks.

I used my Inner Compass to determine if the contractor running this crucial part of the project was on the level. And the answer I got was, "No way!" I tested again—same thing —"Run away from this person!" Over and over I got the same answer.

I reported to my boss that I didn't think this was the right person. He asked me why I thought this, as he'd worked with this person several times before. I wasn't quite ready to come out of the closet with the Inner Compass Method, so I just told him that I had a very strong hunch. He replied that my hunch wasn't a strong enough reason to take her off the job and I would now be responsible for her performance on the production.

There was a lot of drama along the way in supervising this person. So every day I prayed for this person's happiness during my Buddhist practice. But we still fought like cats and dogs, until finally I was able to reflect on her anger and realized she was a deeply troubled person. I stopped letting my negativity feed off of her suffering, and was able to make peace with her. Then, amazingly, she was moved to a different area and given a new boss.

But that wasn't the end of the story...

I later found out she ended up botching her job. She lied about having made a deal with Bob Dylan's production company and the producers had to pay out over $1 million to settle the matter. Her company crashed and my boss later told me that he really wished he'd listened to my "hunch."

Years have gone by and I continue to use my Inner Compass to help me determine the veracity of the stories I hear, the character of the people I am hiring, and even the believability of candidates seeking my vote. But now I'm not afraid to tell people where my insights come from.

Here's how I do it.

When I'm interviewing someone for a potential job, I very subtly place my hand over my heart and with my feet flat on the floor, ask myself silently, "For my highest good and in the greatest service of others, is this a person of high integrity?" If I get a "yes", then I'm on to the next step. If I get a "no", I will usually retest at least two more times. If I keep getting my "no" signal, then for all intents and purposes the interview is over. There may be some more pleasantries, but there's no sense wasting another moment with someone who isn't telling me the truth.

Have I been fooled by people? Absolutely. I once met presidential candidate John Edwards at a fund-raiser. I really enjoyed his speech and even gave him some money. He turned out to be one of the worst liars running for president in quite a while. Why did I get fooled by him? Because he was so likable in person that I never even accessed my Inner Compass to check his stories. I wasn't let down by the process, but instead by my own gullibility!

I don't make that mistake anymore.

Now, when I'm interviewing for a job opening in one of my companies, hiring a contractor, meeting a new business contact or deciding who to vote for in an election, I ask myself these questions—always beginning with the statement,"For my highest good and in the greatest service of others":

- Is this an honorable person of high integrity? If not, game over.
- Is this someone who deserves my trust/vote/business/money (pick one)? If not, adios amigo!

If I get a "yes" to the above questions, then I can begin probing more deeply:

- Is this a person with whom I should do business?
- Is this a good potential partner?
- Is this person someone I could recommend to a friend?
- Is this person someone who follows through on what they say they will do?

- Is this a person who can complete the job on time and on budget?

And so on.

If you think that what I am doing is unfair, that I am judging people without any evidence of their actions and character, I would simply encourage you to try it yourself. I have been experimenting with this process for long enough to guarantee that using your Inner Compass can save you days, months, or even years of heartache, as well as untold thousands of wasted dollars, and prevent you from stressing unnecessarily over things that could have been easily avoided.

If more people knew how to use their Inner Compass when making important decisions or giving their precious trust to others, I truly believe there would be fewer cheats and con-men, fewer divorces and more harmony and joy in the world. When more and more people use their Inner Compass, the Bernie Madoffs, Richard Nixons and Enrons of the future won't stand a chance!

Now you never have to fall victim to these bad apples should they appear in your life. Keep in mind, the more likable the person, the more important it is for you to check them using your Inner Compass. Remember my story about John Edwards? I even gave money to Lance Armstrong's charity once.

Groucho Marx said, "Time wounds all heels." I agree with Groucho that the Law of Cause and Effect eventually catches up with every crook. But why should you have to wait. Why not find out now and navigate safely away from them before they crash the Titanic into an iceberg!

What to do now: Politics as usual

Do the grounding and breathing exercises from the earlier chapter to get centered and clear your mind a bit. Now take out a magazine or newspaper. Place your right index finger on the picture of any politician or government official. They can be local, state, national, international... it doesn't matter. Just pick one person.

Now place your left hand over your heart and say out loud, "For my highest good and in the greatest service to others, is this a person of high integrity?"

What did you get? Are you surprised?

Pick another and repeat.

Turn on the TV or computer and find the picture of a national politician. Ask yourself the above question but this time just point at or touch their image on the screen. Now pick one from a different party than you normally vote for.

What happened?

What to do now: Vetting your circle of trust

After you've experimented with this a few times, perhaps you are ready to do something truly daring. This just might be one of the most courageous acts you've ever done in your life.

Remember, at the beginning of this book, when you filled in a drawing of your trust circles? You are now at the point where you can ask some important questions about the people you have decided are worthy of your trust.

Find the circles of trust image and place your right index finger on one of the names you wrote down. Place your left hand over your heart. Take a couple of deep cleansing breaths and then ask yourself out loud, "For my highest good and in the greatest service to others, is this a person of high integrity?"

Test again at least two more times. If you get a consistent "yes" answer, you may find some real relief in this deep internal knowing. But if you get a "no" answer, you may need to make some changes in your life or at least ask this person some tough questions.

Sometimes you may get your "more info needed" sign or signal. This may mean that you need to rephrase the question. It may also mean that you need to be more specific. I've discovered that some people are reliable in certain areas of their lives but not in others. For example, they may be honest with their friends but be stealing from work. The human mind is complex. Try asking this question, "For my highest good and in the greatest service to others, is [state their full name] worthy of my trust?"

And don't get mad at me if you discover something is afoul in your trust circles. I have had a few unpleasant wake-up calls myself using this process. But am I glad to know the truth? Absolutely!

A wise Buddhist friend used to say that there is no such thing as a bad truth—there may be painful truths, unwelcome truths, and gut-wrenching truths, but the truth is always worth knowing.

And what a relief it is to know that there are people in my life that I can really trust, who I know will hold me accountable and vice versa. If others can discern when I'm slipping into my bullsh*t and call me out on it, I am all the better for it. If I know that I'm being monitored, I'm going to be more on my own game, making sure my nose is clean. Multiply that by thousands or even millions of people and society will change. It may take a while, but in the meantime you won't be bamboozled by hucksters, cheats, con men or politicians seeking to use you for their own personal gain.

What to do now: Speak to the fire

If you are truly courageous, you may be ready for another experiment. If you really want to know what's going on in your life, you owe it to yourself to test some of your deepest beliefs.

Remember our song lyrics, "they taught it, you bought it, but what is your essential truth?" The next time you are in your church, synagogue, temple, mosque or other house of worship, wait until the leader of your religious group starts speaking. Then place your feet flat on the floor, hand on your heart and ask yourself if the person speaking is someone of high integrity. Ask yourself, "Does this person practice what they preach? Are they manipulating or taking advantage of members of their congregation?"

Please understand that I have nothing against organized religion. I've been a member of a religious group for 30 years. Many wonderful people are called to serve through spiritual and religious work. But even in the world of Buddhism, not everyone tells the truth. Sometimes people fall off the path and start putting their hands in the cookie jar or having extra-marital affairs or taking other actions that would put them at odds with the intent of the Buddha.

It happens.

And I think you deserve to know about it.

There are too many people on this planet who have been abused by figures of authority, many of them garbed in religious clothing. I don't want another single person to suffer this way.

Caution: What to do if you get a troubling answer

What do you do if your Inner Compass tells you that there's something amiss? Whether it's in your trust circles, at your church or at work, you now have to make another important set of decisions...

Here's what I ask, "For my highest good, and in the greatest service to others, including the members of my church/company/family, should I take any action based on the information my Inner Compass has given me about [person's full name]?"

If I get a "no", then I retest it. If I get a "no" again, then I will put the matter aside for a few days and ask again. If still get a "no", then I will leave the matter alone until I get the feeling I should ask again. In the meantime, I put the person in question on my watch list and keep my eyes peeled for any suspicious behavior.

If I get a "yes", then I retest it. If I get a "yes" again, I ask my Inner Compass the following question, "For my highest good, and in the greatest service to others, including the members of my church/

company/family, should I remove myself or my children from any contact with [person's full name]?"

If I get a "yes" answer to this question and again after retesting a few times, I make changes immediately. I've actually cancelled deals with people, changed travel plans, walked out on meetings and pulled my kids out of childcare when I got this answer.

This is serious business and I hope you will consider it very carefully. Your life, your career, and the well-being of your loved ones may be at stake.

Concluding Thoughts

I used to think that I was a bit of a freak for doing all these intuition experiments. I thought no one else on the planet was doing anything like this. But I was wrong. Every day, millions of people are getting information from their inner wisdom or intuition.

A few months ago I was speaking at a community service breakfast and asked the audience how many of them had some experience with intuition. To my great surprise, over three quarters of the people in the room shot up their hands – including doctors, lawyers, professors and even the town mayor!

The problem for most folks who get these intuitive "hits" or gut feelings is that they have no way of putting them into context. They just appear out of the blue. And because most people have no way of accessing these feelings on a consistent basis, they never learn how to trust them.

Recently, a friend shared a powerful story that perfectly illustrates the problem with having occasional flashes of intuition.

My friend had studied dance in college, but after graduation she was barely making ends meet. Then she heard about a dance teacher position at a local high school. The job sounded ideal: good pay, attractive benefits, diverse community, and the chance to do what she loved. So she applied. Because the school year was about to start, the school needed someone in a hurry. So when her interview went well, they offered her the job on the spot.

At the end of the interview, the principal asked her if she'd like to see inside the school, which had been shut for most of the summer. My friend said sure, and as the principal unlocked and opened the door, a huge whoosh of stale air rushed out, almost knocking her over. Immediately she felt this terrible urge to leave. Her body physically trembled with the feeling that something was wrong.

But my friend needed the money and she had no way of putting this gut feeling into context. The pros by far outweighed this visceral, but singular, experience. So she took the job.

Within a month, she was already regretting her decision. The school was divided racially and her program got caught up in the animosity. Then one day her supervisor, a respected older man who coached the football team and was head of the Physical Education Department, cornered her in her office and sexually harassed her. When she reported the incident to the principal, she found herself the victim of an ugly smear campaign.

It was the worst year of her life.

She told me that she had known all along not to take the job. The feeling had been so strong – the moment the door opened. But not only did she ignore it; she acted directly counter to her intuition. And she suffered as a result.

This unfortunate story contains a powerful lesson. While there is never an excuse for sexual harassment, racism or other deplorable behavior, unfortunately we live in a world where these situations are a reality for many people. Fortunately, our intuition can be an invaluable tool to help us avoid or minimize these kinds of problems. But even if we have flashes of intuition, if we don't know how to test them, we might not have the confidence to act in our own best interest.

In order to overcome self-doubt and really trust yourself, you need a method or a system for accessing your inner wisdom that is consistent, repeatable and accurate. The Inner Compass Method was created to provide you with just such a process.

By learning to trust your Inner Compass, you can live a life of clarity and confidence. You no longer need to rely on others to decide what is best for you. And you no longer need to fear being manipulated by others who don't have your best interest at heart.

The freedom you can experience by incorporating your Inner Compass into your daily life is hard to describe, but it can make a world of difference. And not only can it make a difference in your world, but the more people who learn to access and trust their Inner Compass, the sooner our entire planet will change for the better.

By learning to access your Inner Compass, you are learning to end self-doubt. And by living a life of clarity and confidence, you can inspire others to do the same. As the Buddha said, "A lamp can illuminate a cave that has been dark for 10,000 years." It's never too late to allow the truth of your own greatness to shine out, and in doing so give hope to countless others.

Afterword

I want to sincerely thank you, not just for reading this book, but also for taking the time to consider what your life might be like if you learned how to end self-doubt. I salute your adventurous spirit, your willingness to try something new, to challenge your existing beliefs and to get outside your comfort zone in search of the truth.

You've learned some innovative and cutting edge techniques and strategies for making even life's toughest decisions quickly and easily. You've discovered how to replace the Inner Critic with your Super Friends group. You identified and began to work with your Inner Compass. And if you were feeling especially courageous, you started asking some deep questions about who deserves your trust and who does not.

I believe that you deserve the very best that life has to offer. And being able to trust yourself is a crucial skill for living a joyful and fulfilling life.

Life is challenging enough as it is, there's no need to suffer unnecessarily when we can navigate through difficult waters using our own Inner Compass.

If you've found value in these processes, I hope you'll consider sharing this work with others. The more people who are able to tap their inner wisdom, access their Inner Compass, and forge a truly authentic path in life, the better our world will be.

And if you'd like to learn more about this work, perhaps even accelerate your skills, I invite you to check out my video e-course, "Decide Now with The Inner Compass Method".[14]

Each year I conduct a limited number of in-person workshops to help my clients strengthen their Inner Compass, discover their Life Direction, and increase their sense of self-confidence. Learning in person can dramatically deepen your understanding and accelerate your abilities, while working in a group gives you the chance to learn new perspectives. To find out when the next workshop is scheduled, please check out our website: www.modernwisdom.com.[15]

If you have any questions, concerns or want to share your success stories, you can reach me at mjs@modernwisdom.com

I wish you every success at work, at home, and in your community. I hope you use these tools to build a palace of joy and fulfillment in your life that you can share with others and create a wave of peace and happiness that envelopes our entire planet.

With warmth and gratitude,

Marc J. Sachnoff

---

14   http://modernwisdom.com/stress-free-decision-making-s1/
15   http://modernwisdom.com/contact-marc-sachnoff/

Resources

Books

- *Feel The Fear and Do It Anyway* by Susan Jeffers. I had the good fortune to meet and dialogue with Susan. She was a true inspiration and has helped thousands of people free themselves from fear.
- *The Buddha in Your Mirror* by Woody Hochswender, Greg Martin and Ted Morino. This is my favorite introduction to Buddhism. It gives you practical information in simple terms that can help you begin your Buddhist practice.
- *Choose Yourself* by James Altucher. I'm really impressed with James's intelligence, curiosity and raw willingness to open his heart and life to his readers. If you want a thought-provoking book on the changes occurring in business and society and how they will impact your life, this is a fast, easy read.
- *Love Yourself Like Your Life Depended on It* by Kamal Ravikant. Kamal's book is an elegantly simple tale of how he saved his own life by loving himself. He shares a powerful practice for experiencing the same deep shift that allowed him to transform from a sick, broke and failed entrepreneur to a happy, healthy and successful businessman.
- *Finding Your North Star* by Martha Beck. Martha combines the process and systems orientation of an organizational develop-

ment nerd with the heart and compassion of a spiritual teacher. Great stuff to compliment your Inner Compass work.

- *7 Spiritual Laws of Success* by Deepak Chopra. Introduced over 20 years ago, this seminal work contains timeless wisdom for anyone seeking to improve their life.
- *Think and Grow Rich* by Napoleon Hill. This guy is my hero. One of the fathers of the personal growth movement, his most famous book has been transforming lives since it was introduced in the 1930s. The language may be dated in some passages, but the message rings true even today.
- *Outwitting the Devil* by Napoleon Hill. This is a book that Hill's family prevented from being published until long after his death. It presents a powerful, but controversial condemnation of the way most people think and act and puts much of the blame on the institutions of society at a time when such questioning would have been considered unpatriotic and heretical.

Techniques

EFT - Emotional Freedom Technique. Created by Gary Craig, this unusually effective process can help you release stuck emotions, overcome fears and phobias, and reduce stress and anxiety. To find a practitioner in your area, check out: http://www.eftuniverse.com/

"Decide Now with The Inner Compass Method" is my video e-course which takes you step by step through the decision-making process used in this book. It is filled with valuable information and techniques and has particular value to business and professional people. You can access it at http://decidenow.modernwisdom.com Enter this promotional code for a special discount: EndofDoubt.

✦

Frequently Asked Questions

Can I choose anyone to be in my Inner Dinner Party?

Yes, you can choose any person, living or dead, real or fictional.

Is the Inner Compass Method the same as muscle testing or using a pendulum?

The purpose of the Inner Compass Method is to help you develop trust in yourself without the need for a muscle testing partner or a tool like a pendulum. While these techniques may be valuable to some people, the ultimate goal is be able to access your inner wisdom directly.

My Inner Compass is not working yet...

If you've tried accessing your Inner Compass and you're not getting anything yet, please take a look at this check list.

1. Am I doing this work in a safe, comfortable location without distraction? If not, please move or delay your experimenting until you can find a suitable place to work. It's important to find a safe, comfortable location where you won't be interrupted or distracted. And please turn off your cell phone.

2. Am I in an agitated emotional state? If so, please take a break; breathe, exercise, talk to a friend or trusted counselor, or even take a hot bath until the emotions subside a bit.

3. Am I physically ill? Do I have a fever, headache, stomachache or other distracting pain? You can achieve results with this work while you are physically sick, but illness is not the optimal condition to begin the process of accessing your Inner Compass. If possible, please rest and allow your body to heal before continuing.

Here are some techniques to consider if you don't think you're getting a clear or consistent signal from your Inner Compass.

Animal Totem Technique

Try this alternate method of finding your "yes" signal. Close your eyes and ask yourself, "What is my favorite animal?" When you ask yourself this question, does a picture of an animal pop into your mind's eye? If so, you can use that picture as your "yes" signal. When asking a question, if the picture of that animal comes into your mind's eye, that's your Inner Compass's way of giving you a "yes" answer.

You can also do this for your "no" signal. Is there an animal that you don't like or are afraid of? Close your eyes and ask yourself "What animal (or insect) do I dislike or find creepy? When you ask yourself this question, does a picture of an animal pop into your mind's eye? If so, you can use that picture as your "no" signal. When asking a question, if the picture of that animal comes into your mind's eye, that's your Inner Compass's way of giving you a "no" answer.

Living Compass Technique

Another simple way to get started is to imagine standing on the face of a compass. Find a quiet room with space to move around and stand straight up. Imagine you are standing at the center of the compass and ask your inner wisdom to "point" you in the direction of "yes", by saying: "For my highest good and in the greatest service of others, please show me what the answer 'yes' to a question feels like by directing my body towards the compass point that signifies 'yes'."

You may feel yourself pulling or leaning towards one of the compass points. A slight tug is all we're looking for but some people may experience a strong pull. Standing lightly on the balls of your feet can also help make you more sensitive to the movement of your Inner Compass.

This just feels weird to me...

That's OK! It's completely natural that something new and unfamiliar to you might feel uncomfortable at first. The most important thing is that you want to try. Having worked with hundreds of people, I can assure you that anyone can do this. And because this is only about working towards your highest good and in the greatest service of others, it cannot hurt you or anyone else. So please rest assured that this is a positive process.

I am a Christian and believe this is against the teachings of Jesus...

Among the hundreds of people I've worked with, many of them were devout Christians. One young woman told that she didn't think Jesus would want her to do these experiments. I asked her if she thought Jesus wanted her to be happy. "Of course," she replied, "Jesus wants everyone to be happy." I asked her if she thought Jesus would want her to be able to discern the honest and true from the duplicitous and false. Again, she agreed.

So we decided to make a customized version that took into account her faith, and it worked beautifully. From then on, she used the following set-up for her questions: "For my highest good, and in the greatest service of others, and in harmony with my love of Jesus..."

Feel free to try this if you think it would make you more comfortable.

Disclaimer

- The material contained in this book is for informational purposes only.
- The author is not a therapist, medical doctor, marriage counselor, lawyer or accountant. You should always seek the advice of a professional before acting on something that the author has published or recommended.
- There are some links contained in this book that the author may benefit from financially.
- The material in this book may include information, products or services by third parties. Third party materials are comprised of the products and opinions expressed by their owners. As such, the author does not assume responsibility or liability for any third party materials or opinions.
- The publication of such third party materials does not constitute the author's guarantee of any information, instruction, opinion, products or services contained within the third party materials. The use of recommended third party materials does not guarantee any success and or results related to you or your business. Publication of such third party materials is simply a recommendation and an expression of the author's opinion of such materials.
- No part of this publication shall be reproduced, transmitted or sold in whole or in part, in any form, without the prior written consent of the author. All trademarks and registered trademarks appearing in this book are the property of their respective owners.
- Users of this book are advised to do their own due diligence when it comes to making business and/or personal decisions and all information, products, and services that have been

provided should be independently verified by qualified professionals.

- Although the author and publisher have made every effort to
ensure that the information in this book was correct at press
time, the author and publisher do not assume and hereby
disclaim any liability to any party for any loss, damage, or dis-
ruption caused by errors or omissions, whether such errors or
omissions result from negligence, accident, or any other cause.

About the Author

Leaders, luminaries, and business owners serious about extraordinary performance rely on Intuitive Business Strategist and Clarity Coach Marc Sachnoff to help them solve thorny problems and discover new opportunities so they can make more money, have more impact, and live with greater confidence and peace of mind.

Called the "King of Clarity" by clients including Microsoft, Precor and Consolidar, Inc, Marc is a transformational catalyst who has helped hundreds of people make life-changing decisions, strengthen their relationships, and realign their companies to stand out from their competition.

Since 2003, Marc has guided leaders to make successful career changes and decisions, evaluate mergers and acquisitions, successfully launch new products, create innovative marketing plans, and find new and profitable markets and products. He has served individuals, companies and teams worldwide through educational keynotes, workshops, online courses, books and one-on-one advisory services.

Bringing strategic, marketing, business development, negotiation and entrepreneurial skills together with acute intuitive, creative, and mindful abilities, Marc offers an unparalleled perspective to leaders of companies and organizations.

A strong believer in the power of personal relationships, Marc brought his intuition, business development, licensing and intellectual property skills to the fledgling start up, WizKids Games, in 2000. Marc's contribution in deal making was recognized as a major catalyst to the company's sale to the Topps Company for $30 million. In his work in Hollywood from 1990 to 2005 on over 150 hours of broadcast television as a writer/director/producer, Marc brought his creative leadership skills to such renowned projects as "Sesame Street's 25th Anniversary," the 10 hour "History of Rock 'N Roll," with Quincy

Jones, and producing the "Bells of Hope Celebration" for the Presidential Inaugural Committee. Awards and recognition followed including two prime time Emmy nominations, a New York Television Festival Gold Award, book awards, and membership in the Writers Guild of America, the Directors Guild of America, and the Academy of Television Arts and Sciences.

Following successful ventures in television production, gaming, marketing, and non-profit leadership, Marc shifted his focus to providing Intuitive Business Strategy consulting and high level personal advisory services to leaders serious about making the wisest and most effective choices that lead to success. What sets Marc apart from other consultants, coaches and trainers is his unique combination of solid business experience and results and 30 years of Buddhist practice.

Marc lives in the Seattle area with his wife, six mechanical pianos, four Victrolas, and a Bernese Mountain Dog named Gatsby.

To work directly with the King of Clarity, book Marc to speak, make quantity purchases of this book, and learn more about his perspective-shifting and proven strategy work, training programs, and the Inner Compass Method, visit www.modernwisdom.com.

MODERN WISDOM

INNER COMPASS METHOD™
Decision Making Worksheet

Name: _____ **Date:** _____

Decision Question: _____

    A) Content _____ B) Context _____ C) Timing _____

Noble Higher Purpose: _____

Expand Options:

    Option #1: _____

    Option #2: _____

    Option #3: _____

    Option #4: _____

Opportunity cost: _____

Research, Data, Expert Advice or Analysis needed: _____

What advice would I give to a friend in the same situation? _____

10/10/10 Questions (Suzy Welch). If I choose:

    How will I feel 10 minutes from executing on this? _____

    How will I feel 10 months from executing on this? _____

    How will I feel 10 years from executing on this? _____

What would have to be true for this to be the right choice? _____

Inner Compass:

    Yes: _____ No: _____

    Need More information: _____

Action will I take today to move forward on my decision? _____

www.ingramcontent.com/pod-product-compliance
Lightning Source LLC
Chambersburg PA
CBHW020513030426
42337CB00011B/372